Extreme Skydiving

EXTREME SPORTS No Limits!

Bobbie Kalman & John Crossingham

Crabtree Publishing Company

www.crabtreebooks.com

Extreme SPORTS No Limits!

Created by Bobbie Kalman

Dedicated by Andrea Crabtree
To Mark, Noah, and Eric
The sky's the limit. Always dive into your dreams. Love, your cousin Andrea

Editor-in-Chief
Bobbie Kalman

Writing team
Bobbie Kalman
John Crossingham

Substantive editor
Kelley MacAulay

Editors
Molly Aloian
Robin Johnson
Rebecca Sjonger
Kathryn Smithyman

Design
Katherine Kantor

Production coordinator
Heather Fitzpatrick

Photo research
Crystal Foxton

Consultant
Tim Grech, Skydiving Instructor
Niagara Skydive Centre Inc.

Illustrations
Bonna Rouse: pages 10, 12

Photographs
© Troy Hartman. Photographed by Vic Pappadato: page 30
photos by Joe Jennings/skydive.com: pages 6-7, 15 (bottom)
Joel Kiesel: pages 5, 13, 20, 21, 26
Mike McGowan/www.funairphotos.com: pages 8, 15 (top),
   16, 17, 18, 19, 22, 23, 24, 25, 28-29, 31
Craig O'Brien/www.craigob.com: page 27
Other images by Digital Vision and Photodisc

Crabtree Publishing Company

www.crabtreebooks.com   1-800-387-7650

Cataloging-in-Publication Data
Kalman, Bobbie.
   Extreme skydiving / Bobbie Kalman & John Crossingham.
      p. cm. -- (Extreme sports no limits!)
   Includes index.
   ISBN-13: 978-0-7787-1684-6 (rlb)
   ISBN-10: 0-7787-1684-8 (rlb)
   ISBN-13: 978-0-7787-1730-0 (pbk)
   ISBN-10: 0-7787-1730-5 (pbk)
   1. Aeronautical sports--Juvenile literature. 2. Extreme sports--
Juvenile literature. I. Crossingham, John. II. Title. III. Series.
   GV755.K34 2006
   797.5--dc22
                                                        2005035791
                                                        LC

**Published in
the United States**

PMB16A
350 Fifth Ave.
Suite 3308
New York, NY
10118

**Published
in Canada**

616 Welland Ave.
St. Catharines, Ontario
L2M 5V6

**Published in the
United Kingdom**

White Cross Mills
High Town, Lancaster
LA1 4XS

**Published
in Australia**

386 Mt. Alexander Rd.
Ascot Vale (Melbourne)
VIC 3032

CONTENTS

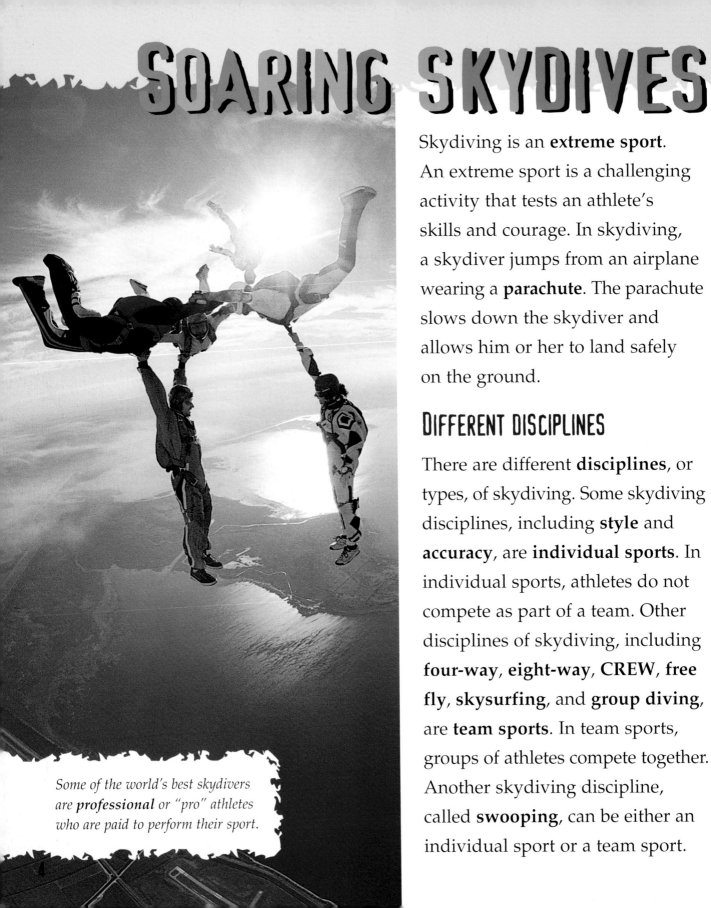

SOARING SKYDIVES

Skydiving is an **extreme sport**. An extreme sport is a challenging activity that tests an athlete's skills and courage. In skydiving, a skydiver jumps from an airplane wearing a **parachute**. The parachute slows down the skydiver and allows him or her to land safely on the ground.

DIFFERENT DISCIPLINES

There are different **disciplines**, or types, of skydiving. Some skydiving disciplines, including **style** and **accuracy**, are **individual sports**. In individual sports, athletes do not compete as part of a team. Other disciplines of skydiving, including **four-way**, **eight-way**, **CREW**, **free fly**, **skysurfing**, and **group diving**, are **team sports**. In team sports, groups of athletes compete together. Another skydiving discipline, called **swooping**, can be either an individual sport or a team sport.

*Some of the world's best skydivers are **professional** or "pro" athletes who are paid to perform their sport.*

Many skydivers jump with **camera fliers**. A camera flier is a skydiver who captures another skydiver's performance on video.

EXTREME DANGER!

Extreme skydiving may be exciting, but it is also very dangerous. All the athletes shown in this book are professionals who have trained for years with expert instructors. Look out below!

DIVE INTO THE PAST

People have been trying to fly for hundreds of years. The invention of hot-air balloons in the late 1700s made it possible for people to leave the ground in huge baskets. Some people wanted more freedom in the air, however. In 1797, a Frenchman named André-Jacques Garnerin made one of the first successful parachute jumps by leaping out of a hot-air balloon over Paris, France.

A WHOLE NEW PLANE

In 1912, people began skydiving from airplanes. Skydivers wore backpacks that contained parachutes. After they jumped from the planes, the skydivers used their hands to pull the parachutes out of their backpacks. With each jump, people learned more about parachutes and how to improve them. In 1918, an American named Leslie Irvin invented a parachute that had a **ripcord**. When they jumped out of planes, skydivers simply pulled the ripcords to release their parachutes.

TIMELINE

1483-1486: Artist Leonardo da Vinci creates one of the first sketches of a parachute.
1885: Thomas Scott Baldwin jumps from a hot-air balloon over San Francisco, becoming the first person in the United States to make a jump.
1890: Paul Letteman and Kathchen Paulus make the first parachute that can be folded up and placed into a backpack.
1922: Test pilot Lieutenant Harold H. Harris makes the first emergency parachute jump from a crashing airplane.
1989: Patrick de Gayardon experiments on **skyboards** in the air, greatly improving the boards and increasing the popularity of the sport.
1990: The World Freestyle Federation (WFF) holds the first international skysurfing competition.

LEARNING TO FALL

Early skydivers pulled their ripcords immediately after jumping from planes. In 1925, however, a group of skydivers waited before pulling their ripcords. These skydivers were the first people to experiment with **free falling**. They found it difficult to control their falls, however. In the late 1940s, a Frenchman named Leo Valentin held his body in a **spread-eagle position** during a free fall. This position helped **stabilize** his body during the fall. **Daredevils** around the world were soon eager to try Valentin's new diving position.

GET ON BOARD

By the 1980s, skydiving was popular worldwide. Skydivers had mastered individual free falls and were jumping together in large groups. In 1987, a French diver named Joel Cruciani put **bindings** on a surfboard and became the first skysurfer. The large surfboard was difficult to control, however, so people tried using skateboards and, eventually, snowboards during their jumps. By 1992, companies began making skyboards, or boards that were specially designed to allow skydivers to "surf" in the air.

PLANE TO SEE

Although some skydivers leap from helicopters, most jump from airplanes called **jump planes**. A jump plane is a plane that is set up for skydiving. The plane has a large, open **cabin**, or inside compartment. It also has a wide door from which skydivers can jump. The door is usually located on the side of the plane, near the back. The plane may also have a **tailgate**, or a door located at the rear of the plane.

Most jump planes hold between 4 and 23 skydivers. The skydivers sit on benches that are along the inside walls of the plane, or they sit on the floor. When it is time to jump, the skydivers release their seatbelts and walk to the door. If they are performing as a team, all the members of the team jump from the plane at the same time. If they are performing individually, they jump from the plane one at a time.

THE PERFECT SPOT

The **airspace**, or the place in the sky, where skydivers jump from the plane is called the **spot**. Skydivers choose the spot based on the wind conditions in the area. Skydivers performing different disciplines jump at different **altitudes**, or heights. For example, swooping is done at a lower altitude than the altitude at which free flying is done. Most skydivers jump when they are between 3,000 and 13,500 feet (914-4115 m) above the ground. The area on the ground where skydivers land is called the **landing area**.

THE GEAR

Skydiving is an extreme sport that comes with extreme risks! Skydivers need a lot of **gear**, or equipment, to help them perform their daring sport safely.

Goggles keep wind out of a skydiver's eyes.

*Most skydivers wear **helmets** to protect their heads. Many skydiving helmets have **audible altimeters**. An audible altimeter is programmed by a skydiver to beep when he or she reaches certain altitudes.*

*Skydivers wear **jumpsuits** when they dive. Some jumpsuits have extra fabric beneath the arms that act as wings in the air.*

Many skydivers wear gloves made of thin material.

*All skydivers wear **altimeters** on their wrists or chests. These altimeters show how high above the ground the skydivers are.*

Skydivers wear sport shoes.

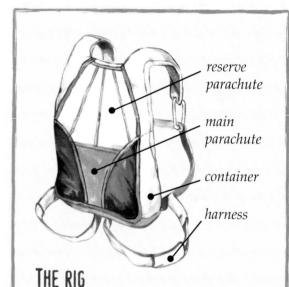

reserve parachute

main parachute

container

harness

THE RIG

An important part of a skydiver's gear is the **rig**. The rig includes a **container**, which holds the **main parachute**, or the parachute the skydiver will use. The container also holds a **reserve parachute**, which is an extra parachute that can be used if the main parachute fails to open. The rig is attached to the skydiver by a set of straps called a **harness**. A rig can cost over $6,000! Skydivers check their rigs before each jump to make sure they are working properly.

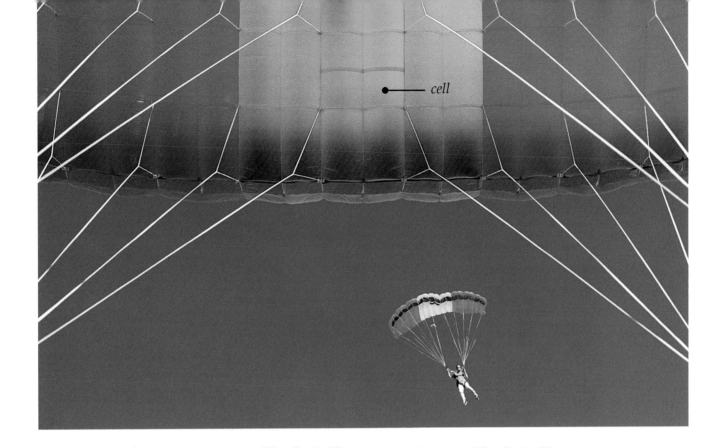

cell

THE PARACHUTE

Most skydivers use **ram-air parachutes**. A ram-air parachute is rectangular in shape and consists of tubes of material called **cells**. This type of parachute is designed to act as a wing, allowing the skydiver to glide easily even in strong winds. To steer their parachutes in different directions, skydivers pull handles on their ram-air parachutes.

RIG IT!

A skydiver rarely has to use his or her reserve parachute. When the reserve parachute is used, it must be repacked by an expert called a **rigger**. To ensure the reserve parachute stays in good condition, a rigger must open, inspect, and repack the parachute every 120 days.

AUTOMATIC DEPLOYMENT

A skydiver's rig has many features that help prevent accidents. One of the most important safety features is the **Automatic Activation Device** (AAD). The AAD is a piece of equipment that is connected to the reserve parachute. A skydiver programs the AAD to **deploy**, or open, the reserve parachute at a certain altitude if the main parachute has not opened.

THE EYE IN THE SKY

Camera fliers are part of many skydiving teams. The camera flier records the actions of the other skydivers on his or her team. There is more to this athlete's job than recording jumps on a camera, however! Camera fliers are expert skydivers who can control their movements perfectly.

camera

ring sight

For added control during their free falls, many camera fliers have large fabric wings underneath the arms of their jumpsuits. These wings help the camera fliers slow down and capture great shots.

HEADGEAR

The camera flier uses a small camera that weighs between one and two pounds (0.4-0.9 kg). The camera is attached to the camera flier's helmet. This setup allows the flier's arms to be free during a dive. A camera flier also usually wears a **ring sight** over one eye. A ring sight is a **transparent**, or see-through, piece of equipment that helps the camera flier aim the camera at other skydivers.

TEAMWORK

Camera fliers sometimes perform **tricks**, or moves, with their teammates. Skydivers and camera fliers practice their tricks many times. By practicing, the camera flier learns how to position the camera in order to capture the best shots.

This camera flier is part of a skysurfing team. He is holding the end of his teammate's skyboard. Performing tricks such as this one during competitions shows the judges that the team is skilled and has good control.

FREE FALLING

Many skydivers enjoy the speed and freedom they experience during free falls. A free fall begins when a skydiver jumps from a plane and ends when the skydiver deploys his or her parachute. During a free fall, two forces are working against each other—**gravity** and **relative wind**. Gravity is the force that pulls a diver down toward Earth.

Relative wind is the rushing air that pushes against the falling diver. It is caused by the diver moving quickly through the air. Relative wind helps slow down the diver's fall. It is also called **wind resistance**.

Relative wind is the force that is pushing up this diver's hair.

FREE-FALL POSITIONS

Skydivers free fall at speeds of over 120 miles per hour (193 kph)! The top speed at which a diver falls is called **terminal velocity**. At terminal velocity, relative wind is very strong. Skydivers position their bodies in different ways as they fall. The different positions help them use relative wind to slow down, speed up, or change direction. For example, to dive quickly, divers hold their arms against their bodies and press their legs together. To slow their dives, skydivers spread out their arms and legs in **box position**. The fabric wings on skydivers' jumpsuits slow them down even more. When the fabric is spread out, it pushes against the relative wind.

To speed up, a diver can fall with his or her head toward the ground. In this upside-down position, a diver's body travels quickly through the air.

In box position, a diver's body is supported by the air.

15

STYLE FOR MILES

Style is an individual discipline of skydiving. In style competitions, a skydiver jumps from a plane at an altitude of about 7,500 feet (2286 m). Once in the air, the diver performs a series of **choreographed**, or preplanned, movements. Every skydiver performs the same movements. Style is a timed competition, so the skydiver who performs the movements in the shortest amount of time wins the competition. To avoid **penalties**, however, the skydiver must perform precise, controlled movements during his or her performance.

KEEPING WATCH

A group of five judges scores a style competition. The judges watch each diver's performance from the ground, using special high-powered **binoculars** called **telemeters**. Many style competitors perform impressive **acrobatic** moves. If the skydivers do not perform each move perfectly, the judges give the skydivers penalties. The penalty is extra time that is added to the skydivers' final score.

By using telemeters, judges on the ground can see how this skydiver is moving her body in the air.

17

HITTING THE MARK

Accuracy is one of the oldest skydiving disciplines. Accuracy competitions are challenging events that test a skydiver's ability to land on a specific mark. In an accuracy competition, skydivers jump from a plane, one at a time, at about 2,800 feet (853 m). As soon as a skydiver has left the plane, he or she opens the parachute and begins maneuvering toward the landing area.

TARGET PRACTICE

An accuracy competitor must aim to land on a big pad that is shaped like a bull's eye. The skydiver must land as close as possible to an **electronic recording disc** in the center of the bull's eye. The disc measures the diver's distance from the center of the bull's eye. Each diver performs a number of jumps. The diver with the smallest combined distance at the end of the event wins.

TINY TARGETS

As skydiving equipment and parachutes have improved over the years, divers have been able to control their landings better. As the landings have become more accurate, the landing discs have become smaller to increase the challenge. In some competitions, the disc is only about two inches (5 cm) wide!

19

SWOOP DOWN FROM THE SKY

Swooping is a skydiving discipline that tests a skydiver's ability to control a ram-air parachute. In swooping competitions, divers fly as close to the ground as possible for as long as they can. The swooper must also guide his or her parachute to a marked area on the ground.

The divers are judged on their style, accuracy, and the distance they can glide. Swooping can be either an individual sport or a team sport. When swooping is a team sport, the team members perform one at a time. The scores of the team members are then added together to get a total.

FLYING LOW

Swoopers jump from about 2,500 feet (762 m). The divers deploy their parachutes as soon as they leave the plane. To build up speed, the skydivers angle the parachutes out in front of their bodies. As the divers near the ground, they pull their parachutes back over their heads to slow the descent.

WALKING ON WATER

Swooping competitions often take place over calm bodies of water, such as ponds. As the skydivers glide over the smooth surface of the water, they sometimes drag their feet lightly through the water to create waves called **rooster tails**. By making rooster tails, the skydivers add bonus marks to their final scores.

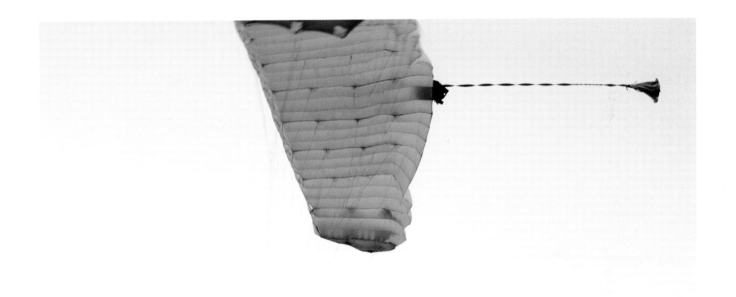

While swooping, divers can reach speeds of 40 miles per hour (64 kph)!

FAB FOURS AND CRAZY EIGHTS

Team skydiving requires skydivers to work together and to communicate well. Two common team disciplines are four-way and eight-way. Four-way teams are made up of five members, and eight-way teams are made up of nine members. The extra member on each team is a camera flier who records the team's performances. Four-way and eight-way skydivers create **formations** as they free fall. These athletes are sometimes known as **belly fliers** because their stomachs often face the ground as they fall.

Performing with a team of divers requires a lot of training. Four-way and eight-way teams practice by jumping many times a day.

FORMING THE MOVES

Four-way and eight-way teammates often create formations by holding one another's arms and legs. Sometimes the teammates join hands to form a cross or a star. The skydivers can hold any parts of their teammates' bodies to make a formation. They often hold one another's ankles, thighs, shins, waists, or shoulders.

TIMED PERFORMACES

Each team in a four-way or an eight-way competition must perform the same moves. Four-way teams jump from about 10,500 feet (3200 m). They have 35 seconds to complete the series. Eight-way teams jump from about 13,000 feet (3962 m). These teams have 50 seconds to complete the series. If a team finishes the series before the 35 seconds are up, they start the series again. A camera flier records the moves for the judges on the ground.

Judges score four-way and eight-way teams on skills such as how gracefully they move from one formation to the next and whether or not they complete the series.

23

CREW MEMBERS

CREW divers must move quickly and smoothly to perform many formations. This image shows a camera flier filming a CREW team as they get into a formation.

CREW stands for Canopy Relative Work. "Canopy" is another name for a parachute. Most CREW teams consist of four skydivers. CREW divers jump at an altitude of about 7,000 feet (2134 m). CREW divers do not free fall. Instead, they open their parachutes as soon as they jump and use them to maneuver into group formations. In the air, the four divers create as many formations as possible. The divers must complete their formations in ninety seconds.

STACK 'EM UP!

The most common CREW formation is the **stack**. In a stack, the divers float one above the other. The team can change the formation by having the top diver steer down to the bottom of the stack. The team continues this motion as often as it can within the time limit.

UNDER CONTROL

CREW skydivers must be skilled at handling their parachutes. Midair collisions and tangled parachutes are two common dangers that CREW divers face. These divers must have perfect control of their ram-air parachutes to perform a stack. **Turbulence**, or high-wind disturbances in the air, can also make it difficult to perform CREW formations. The wind makes the parachutes harder to control.

FREEDOM FLIGHT

Free flying is a discipline that brings a creative side to skydiving. Unlike a four-way or a style diver, a free-fly diver has the chance to experiment with different moves every time he or she dives. This type of discipline is similar to skateboarding, in which athletes are always inventing new moves. Most free-fly teams are made up of two divers and one camera flier.

Free-fly divers perform whatever moves feel most exciting at that moment. A team of free fliers dives out of a plane headfirst to gain the speed they need to perform wild tricks such as **spins**. Free fliers jump at 13,000 feet (3962 m) and have 45 seconds to complete their moves. Judges score divers based on their creativity and on the difficulty of their moves.

BOARDING CALL

The invention of the skyboard introduced a new discipline to the sport of skydiving—skysurfing. Skyboards allow skydivers to ride relative wind in the same way that surfers ride waves. Controlling skyboards isn't easy, however. Even skilled skydivers find it difficult to maintain their balance on skyboards at first.

THAT'S TRICKY!

Skysurfers perform thrilling tricks during competitions. A skysurfing team is made up of a skysurfer and a camera flier. Judges score each skysurfing team on more than just the variety of the tricks or the overall performance. The camera flier must also get the best possible images of the skysurfer's tricks. The best teams use moves that involve both members.

THE HENHOUSE SURPRISE

The **henhouse surprise**, shown above, is a breathtaking skysurfing trick. To perform a henhouse surprise, the skysurfer leans back and grabs the **tail**, or back end, of the skyboard. He or she then spins while falling upside down. Like all skysurfing tricks, the henhouse surprise requires a skysurfer to have perfect balance and control over his or her board.

GROUP SHOT

For skydivers, group diving offers fun new ways to experience free falling. Group skydiving also presents new challenges to skydivers, such as holding one another's hands and legs to create different formations. Most free falls last only 50 to 60 seconds, so all the skydivers must be skilled enough to get into their positions quickly. Formations can be made by as few as four skydivers, or by large groups with over three hundred skydivers who are all linked together!

CAREFULLY PLANNED

When creating a formation in the air, skydivers do not just randomly grab the nearest free diver. During group dives, there is a great risk of midair collisions between skydivers. The pattern of the formation is carefully planned and practiced before the skydivers ever leave the ground. Practicing on the ground is called **dirt diving**. During the dive, each skydiver knows with whom he or she is supposed to link up. Groups of skydivers must leave the plane in a certain order. For large formations, skydivers may have to leap out of many jump planes at once!

This group formation is made up of 300 people!

STARS IN THE SKY

The many disciplines of skydiving have produced some incredible athletes. These fearless divers train tirelessly to improve their skills and increase the popularity of skydiving. These pages include just a few of the skydivers who have had an impact on their sport.

JOE JENNINGS

American camera flier Joe Jennings has been skydiving for over 20 years. In that time, he has won numerous competitions, including two World Skysurfing Championships. Jennings has filmed skydivers for their parts in many movies and commercials. In 1997, he even filmed former President George Bush's first attempt at skydiving! Jennings now owns his own production company and films skydiving for a living.

TROY HARTMAN

Troy Hartman, shown right, is an American skydiver and skysurfer from California who has made over 4,000 jumps! After his first jump in 1991, Hartman was hooked! Since then, his daring skydiving and skysurfing stunts have been featured in many movies, TV shows, and commercials. In 1997, he took home the gold medal in the X-Games skysurfing competition. Hartman's thrill-seeking ways are sure to keep him at the top of his sport for years to come.

TANYA GARCIA-O'BRIEN AND CRAIG O'BRIEN

Americans Tanya Garcia-O'Brien and Craig O'Brien, shown above, make up one of the most successful skydiving teams. Tanya is one of the best skysurfers in the world, and her husband Craig is the camera flier who films her jumps. Their team, which is called Perris Valley Firestarter, has won many skydiving awards and championships. They have been skydiving full-time since 1997. Before that, Craig worked as an electrician, and Tanya worked as a second-grade teacher! Now they work as stunt doubles in movies and television.

MISSY NELSON

American free flier Missy Nelson has been skydiving for almost 25 years. Her father, Roger Nelson, was also an amazing skydiver who helped advance the sport. Missy made her first jump with her father when she was only five years old! She is now a professional skydiving instructor who continues to push the limits of free flying!

KAREN "KAZ" SHEEKEY

Australian-born swooper Karen "Kaz" Sheekey started skydiving in 1993 and swooping in 1997. She joined the Team Fastrax swooping team in 2002. Sheekey placed second overall in the final standings of the 2005 Pro Swooping Tour, making her the highest-ranked female swooper in history!

GLOSSARY

Note: Boldfaced words that are defined in the text may not appear in the glossary.

accuracy A skydiving discipline in which skydivers attempt to land in the middle of a bull's eye

acrobatic Describes moves that require great skill and flexibility to perform

binding Equipment that attaches an athlete's feet to a skyboard, snowboard, or to skis

binoculars A device that makes distant objects appear closer and larger

daredevil A person who participates in risky, adventurous activities

CREW A skydiving discipline in which a team of skydivers uses its parachutes to create formations

eight-way A skydiving discipline in which a team of eight athletes creates formations in the air while free falling

formation A pattern or shape created when skydivers hold on to one another as they free fall

four-way A skydiving discipline in which a team of four athletes creates formations in the air while free falling

free fall The part of a skydive that begins when a diver leaves the plane and ends when the diver releases his or her parachute

free fly A skydiving discipline in which a team of athletes performs tricks in the air

group diving A skydiving discipline in which a large group of divers creates formations in the air

parachute Equipment made of a fabric canopy and ropes that slows a skydiver's fall through the air

penalty A deduction given to an athlete for breaking a rule or performing badly

ripcord A cord pulled to release a parachute

skysurfing A skydiving discipline in which a skydiver rides a skyboard through the air

spin A trick in which a diver rotates in the air

spread-eagle position A position in which the arms and legs are stretched out to the sides

stabilize To make something balanced and stable

style A skydiving discipline in which athletes perform a pre-arranged set of moves while free falling

swooping A skydiving discipline in which a skydiver flies along the ground for as long as possible

INDEX

1 2 3 4 5 6 7 8 9 0 Printed in the U.S.A. 5 4 3 2 1 0 9 8 7 6